ELVIS PRESLEY

07 08 09 10 11 IMA 10 9 8 7 6 5 4 3 2 1

ISBN-13: 978-0-7407-6359-5
ISBN-10: 0-7407-6359-8

Library of Congress Control Number: 2006931985

Produced by Essential Works
www.essentialworks.co.uk

Designed by Kate Ward

www.andrewsmcmeel.com

Attention: Schools and Businesses

inspirations

ELVIS PRESLEY

**Andrews McMeel
Publishing, LLC**

Kansas City

Rhythm is something you either have or don't have,

but when you have it,

you have it all over.

A live concert to me is exciting

because of all the electricity that is generated in the crowd and onstage. It's my favorite part of the business—live concerts.

The first time that I appeared onstage, it scared me to death.

I really didn't know what all the yelling was about.

I didn't realize that my body was moving.

It's a natural thing to me.

So to the manager backstage I said . . .

"What'd I do?"

at'd I do?"

And he said . . .

"Whatever it is . . .

go back &

do it again."

Man, I was tame compared to what they do now.

Are you kidding?

I didn't do anything but just jiggle.

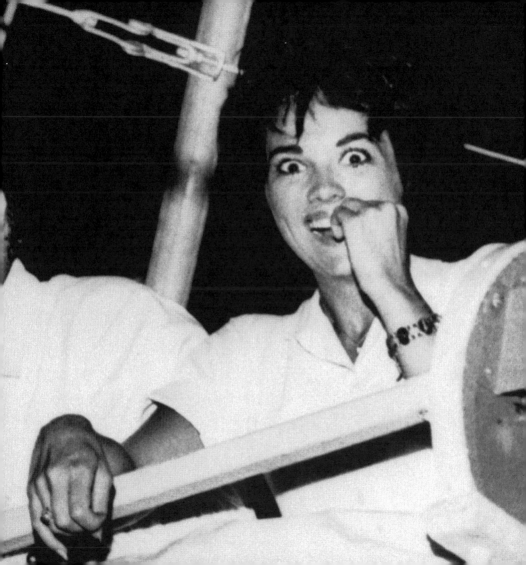

Truth is like the sun.

You can shut it out for a time, but it ain't goin' away.

WHEN THINGS GO WRONG DON'T GO WITH THEM.

I don't

know anything about music.

In my line you don't have to.

I have
no use for
bodyguards

but I have a very
special use for
two highly trained
certified public
accountants.

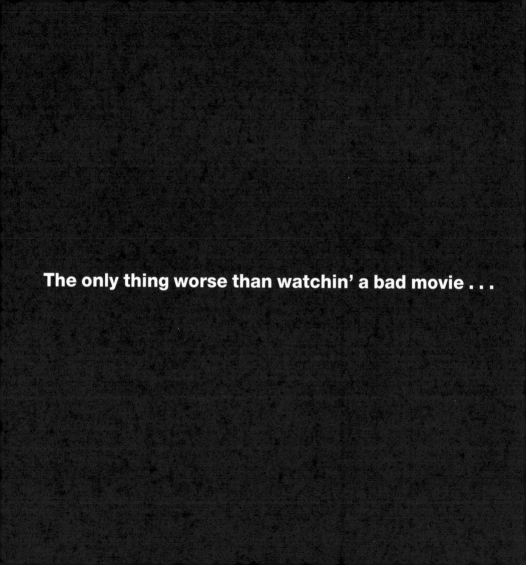

The only thing worse than watchin' a bad movie . . .

is bein' in one.

People who read

into my music

have dirty minds.

Everything happened so blamed fast

I don't know where I was yesterday . . .

and I don't know wl

Sure, they tear off my clothes, they scratch their

initials on my cars, they phone my hotel all night . . .

but they buy my records and they pay to see me sing.

I'm grateful . . .

and when they stop annoying me, I'll start to worry.

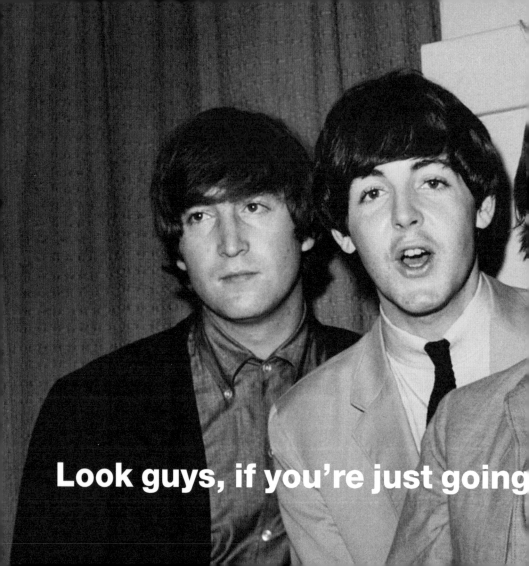

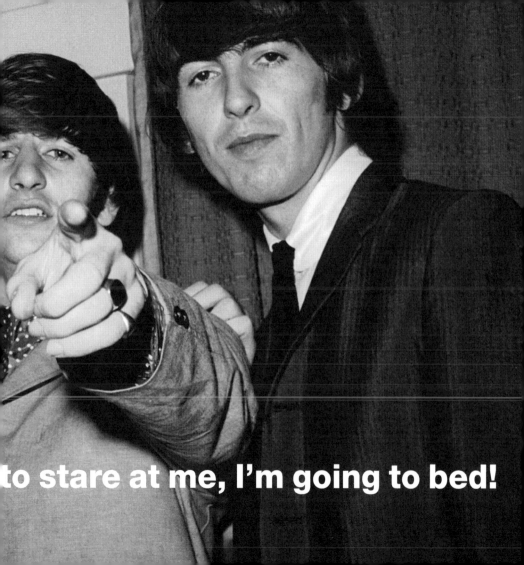
...to stare at me, I'm going to bed!

I DON'T THINK
A FELLOW TO

T'S RIGHT FOR

DRESS LOUD.

ON THE STREET THAT IS . . .

ON THE STAGE, I WANT TO

STAND OUT.

THE LOUDER MY CLOTHES, THE BETTER.

Gospel music is the purest thing there is on this earth.

I don't know

how long the music will last.

I knew by heart all the dialogue of James Dean's films;

I could watch
Rebel Without a Cause

100

times over.

Ambition is a drea

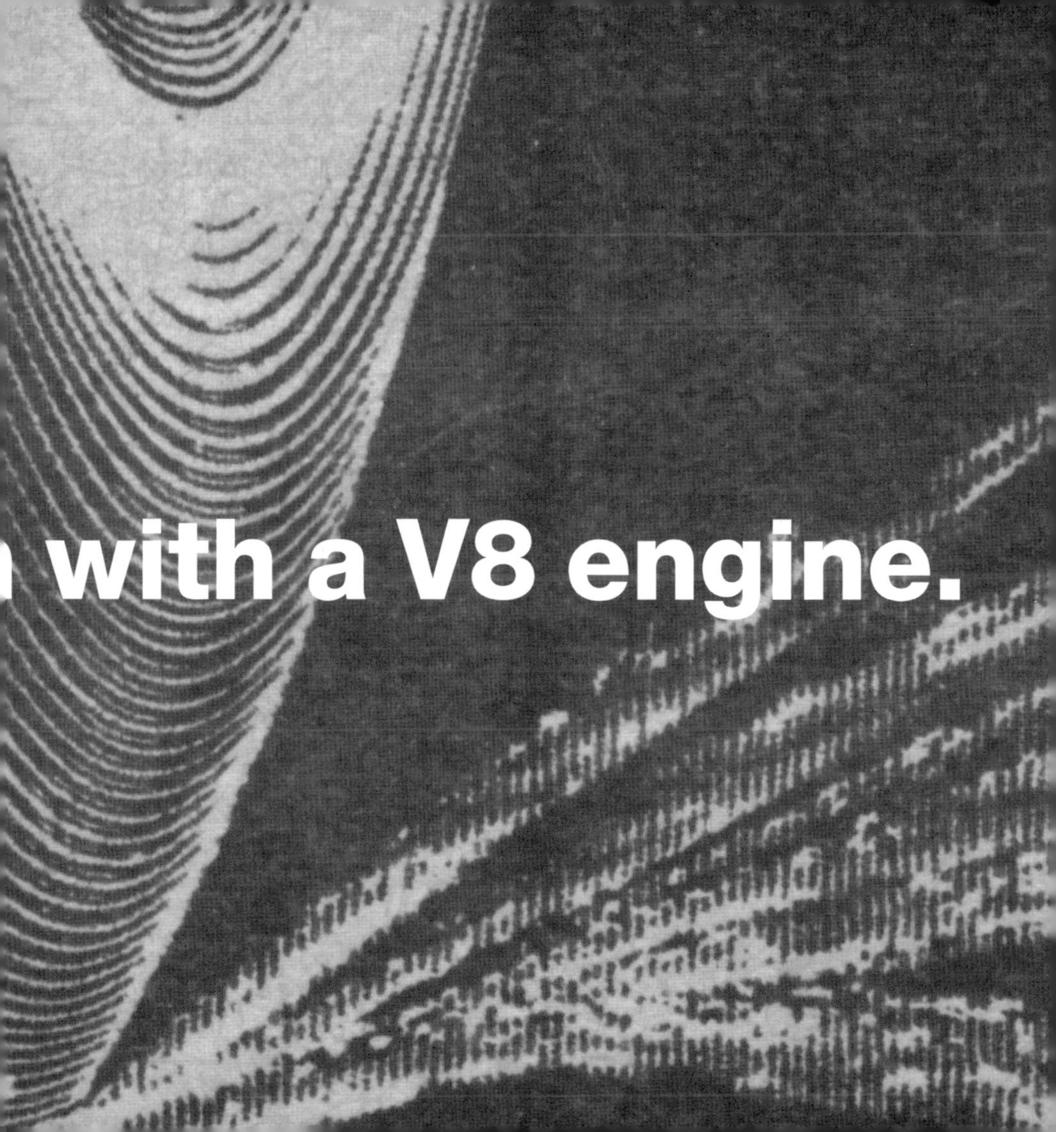
with a V8 engine.

When you let your head get too big . . .

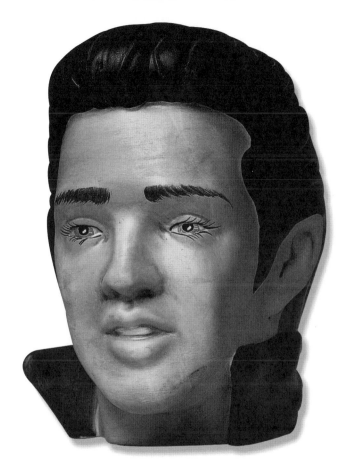

it'll break your neck.

I wasn't ready for that town

and they weren't ready for me.

How many times can you sing about girls,

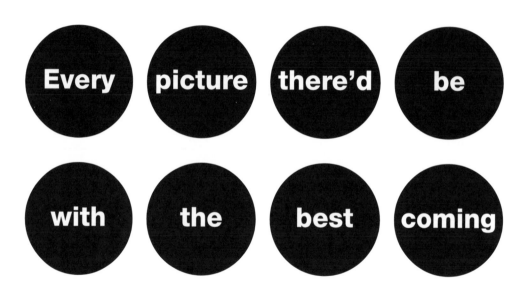

Every picture there'd be

with the best coming

Army days, things like that?

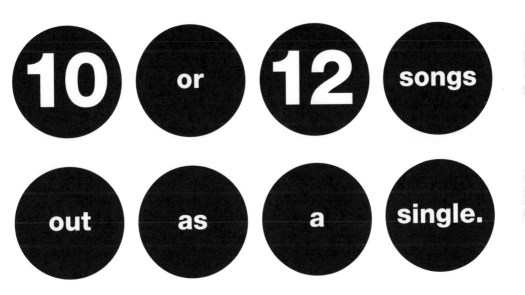

10 or 12 songs out as a single.

There was no way they could all be good.

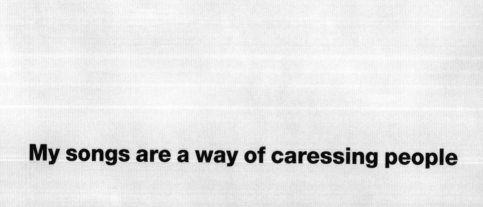

My songs are a way of caressing people

. . . with my voice.

Ain't nowhere else in the world

where you can go from driving a truck to driving a Cadillac overnight.

THIS

is the greatest thing that has happened to me.

I don't believe that death is the end.

Reincarnation has gotta be real.

Just because you look good don't mean you feel good.

TAL
IS BEIN' ABLE TO SELL

ENT

WHAT YOU'RE FEELING.

You can't breathe or even go to the bathroom without them knowin' about it.

How would rock 'n' roll music make anybody rebel against their parents?

I'm sort of getting tired

of being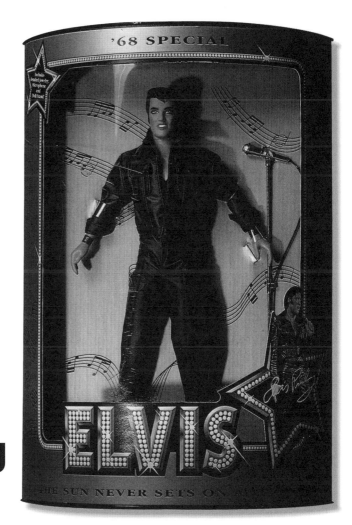

When I was a child, ladies and gentlemen, I was a dreamer. I read comic books, and I was the hero of the comic book. I saw movies, and I was the hero in the movie.

So every dream I ever dreamed

has come true a hundred times.

I don't like being called

THE PE EL

.VIS.

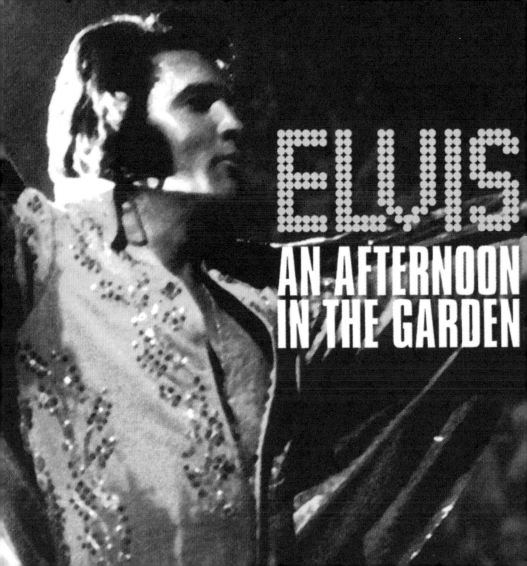

**As long as there's a public,
as long as you're pleasing people,**

it'd be foolish to quit.

I'm still afraid to this day that one morning I'll wake up and find out that everything was a dream and that we're all still back in Tupelo with no hope of getting out from under the poverty.

THE IMAGE
IS ONE THING

AND THE HUMAN
BEING IS ANOTHER.

IT'S VERY HARD TO
LIVE UP TO AN IMAGE.

If I wasn't sincere, I'd just leaf through my work and say . . .

"Gimme my money and I'll get the hell out."

**The world is more alive at night;
it's like God ain't looking.**

Hollywood had lost sight of the basics. They're a lot of fancy talkers who like to pigeonhole you.

I didn't
know what
I wanted
to do as
a kid.
But
I used
to pray
to God
that I'd
amount to
something
some day.

ELVIS The Memphis Record EXTRA

DIGITALLY REMASTERED

1969: YEAR IN REVIEW

COMEBACK Elvis Presley as he appeared in December, 1968 NBC television special.

ACADEMY AWARD WINNERS

- Best Picture — Midnight Cowboy
- Best Actor — John Wayne, True Grit
- Best Actress — Maggie Smith, The Prime Of Miss Jean Brodie
- Best Supporting Actor — Gig Young, They Shoot Horses, Don't They?
- Best Supporting Actress — Goldie Hawn, Cactus Flower

GRAMMY WINNERS

- Record Of The Year — Aquarius/Let The Sunshine In, 5th Dimension
- Album Of The Year — Blood, Sweat & Tears, Blood, Sweat & Tears
- Song Of The Year — Games People Play, Joe South
- Best New Artist — Crosby, Stills And Nash

THE YEAR'S NO. 1 HITS

I Heard It Through The Grapevine – Marvin Gaye
Crimson And Clover – Tommy James & The Shondells
Everyday People – Sly & The Family Stone
Dizzy – Tommy Roe
Aquarius/Let The Sunshine In – 5th Dimension
Get Back – Beatles
Love Theme From "Romeo & Juliet" – Henry Mancini
In The Year 2525 – Zager & Evans
Honky Tonk Women – Rolling Stones
Sugar, Sugar – Archies
I Can't Get Next To You – Temptations
Suspicious Minds – Elvis Presley
Wedding Bell Blues – 5th Dimension
Come Together – Beatles
Na Na Hey Hey Kiss Him Goodbye – Steam
Leaving On A Jet Plane – Peter, Paul and Mary
Someday We'll Be Together – Diana Ross & The Supremes

-ELVIS PRESLEY-
COMMEMORATIVE
ISSUE

- **PRESLEY RETURNS HOME FOR FIRST MEMPHIS SESSIONS SINCE MID-1950's**
- **FIRST MAN WALKS ON MOON**
- **HALF MILLION IN ATTENDANCE AT WOODSTOCK FESTIVAL**
- **NEW YORK METS WIN WORLD SERIES**
- **NIXON SWORN IN AS NATION'S 37TH PRESIDENT**
- **JETS UPSET COLTS IN SUPER BOWL III**

MUSICIANS

RCA

BAND
Reggie Young, guitar; Bobby Wood, piano; Bobby Emmons, organ; Tommy Cogbill, Mike Leech, bass; Gene Chrisman, drums; Ed Kollis, harmonica; John Hughey, steel guitar. Additional piano by Ronnie Milsap (C-1) and Elvis Presley (B-7, B-4).

BACKING VOCALS
Mary Greene, Mary Holladay, Susan Pilkington, Donna Thatcher, Sandy Posey (C-3) and Ronnie Milsap (D-4) in Memphis.
Joe Babcock, Delores Edgin, Millie Kirkham, Sonja Montgomery and Hurshel Wiginton in Nashville (C-2, C-3, D-2, D-4).

HORNS
Wayne Jackson, Dick Steff, R.F. Taylor, trumpets; Andrew Love, J.P. Luper, Glen Spreen, Jackie Thomas, saxophones; Jack Hale, Ed Logan, Gerald Richardson, Jackie Thomas, trombones; Tony Cason, Joe D'Gerolamo, french horns, in Memphis. Norman Prentice, Bobby Shew, Art Vasquez, trumpets; Kenneth Atkins, Johnny Boisot, Archie Le Coque, trombones, in Las Vegas (A-5).

STRINGS
Arnid Blumberg, Albert Edelman, Nate Evans, Ed Friedberg, Noel Gilbert, Gloria Hendricks, Anne Oldham, Hal Saunders, Robert Snyder, Ann Sparfvent, violins; Mike Leech, Fred Lewing, Nino Rasanno, Marv Snyder, Glen Spreen, Vernon Taylor, John Weltur, violas; Pamela Blackwell, Anne Kendall, Joshua Langlur, Peter Spurbeck, cellos in Memphis.
Brenton Banks, George Binkley, Solie Fott, Lillian Hunt, Pierre Menard, Akira Nagai, violins; Martin Chausy, Gary Vanosdale, violas; Byron Bach, Sadau Harada, cellos, in Nashville (C-2, C-3, D-2, D-4).

CONTENTS

1. STRANGER IN MY OWN HOME TOWN (P. Mayfield) 4:39
2. POWER OF MY LOVE (B. Giant/B. Baum/F. Kaye) 2:36
3. ONLY THE STRONG SURVIVE (K. Gamble/L. Huff/J. Butler) 2:42
4. ANY DAY NOW (B. Bacharach/B. Hilliard) 2:59
5. SUSPICIOUS MINDS (M. James) 3:24
6. LONG BLACK LIMOUSINE (V. Stovall/B. George) 3:39
7. WEARIN' THAT LOVED ON LOOK (D. Frazier/A.L. Owens) 2:42
8. I'LL HOLD YOU IN MY HEART (TILL I CAN HOLD YOU IN MY ARMS) (T. Dilbeck/V. Horton/E. Arnold) 4:32
9. AFTER LOVING YOU (E. Miller/J. Lantz) 2:56
10. RUBBERNECKIN' (D. Jones/R. Warren) 2:08
11. I'M MOVIN' ON (H. Snow) 2:55
12. GENTLE ON MY MIND (J. Hartford) 3:19
13. TRUE LOVE TRAVELS ON A GRAVEL ROAD (D. Frazier/A.L. Owens) 2:44
14. IT KEEPS RIGHT ON A-HURTIN' (J. Tillotson) 2:38
15. YOU'LL THINK OF ME (M. Shuman) 4:09
16. MAMA LIKED THE ROSES (J. Christopher) 2:32
17. DON'T CRY DADDY (M. Davis) 2:48
18. IN THE GHETTO (M. Davis) 2:46
19. THE FAIR IS MOVING ON (D. Fletcher/D. Flett) 3:06
20. INHERIT THE WIND (E. Rabbitt) 3:11
21. KENTUCKY RAIN (E. Rabbitt/D. Heard) 3:15
22. WITHOUT LOVE (THERE IS NOTHING) (D. Small) 2:55

For the most band at the city American Studio at 827 Thomas St. in a run-down section of Memphis, it wasn't any big deal. Monday, January 13, marked the beginning of yet another session for yet another artist evidently working the American magic. It was 1969, and the studio was in the midst of a string of 122 chart hits that would be cut over a period of three years with virtually the same rhythm section (Reggie Young on guitar, Bobby

Wood and Bobby Emmons on keyboards, Tommy Cogbill and Mike Leech on bass, Gene Chrisman on drums). Neil Diamond had just finished a session there in the course of which he had recorded "Brother Love's Traveling Salvation Show," "Sweet Caroline," and "Holly Holy." Even if the next artist had not been noted in a long-standing commercial slump, it was difficult at this point to tell just what he was capable of since he had been cut off from concert work the public and his fellow musicians for so long. Everyone in the studio knew who the singer was, they had all grown up on his music, and he was, of course, a native Memphian. But perhaps for these reasons, too, it

seemed as if this session could represent little more than a nostalgia bow to the past. "I mean, we were thrilled about Elvis," said horn player Wayne Jackson, "but it wasn't like doing Neil Diamond."

For Chips Moman, American's founder, owner, chief engineer, songwriter, and occasional guitar player, the upcoming session promised as many headaches as thrills. Like the house band, he knew of and admired Elvis ("I had met him, but that's all— I had been around Memphis for a long time"), but he was also aware that no one had really "produced" an Elvis session in years, and he himself ... *(Full story inside.)*

CREDITS

Recorded at American Studios Memphis, Tennessee
January and February, 1969
Original Sessions Produced by Chips Moman
Arranged by Glen Spreen and Mike Leech
Some Overdubs Produced by Felton Jarvis
Nashville Session Arranged by Don Tweedy
Engineer: Al Pachucki
Assisted by Roy Shockley
This Compilation
A&R Director: Gregg Geller
Mastering Director: Don Wardell
Audio Restoration by Rick Rowe
Mastered by Jack Adelman
Liner Notes by Peter Guralnick
Art Direction: Ria Lewerke
Design: Pierre Affari
Photos courtesy of Michael Ochs Archives

TROUBLE Elvis Presley as he appeared in the 1968 feature "The Trouble With Girls (And How To Get Into It)"

I never dreamed that something like this would happen.

Music is like religion. When you exp

ence them both it should

move you.

Adversity is sometimes hard upon a man . . .

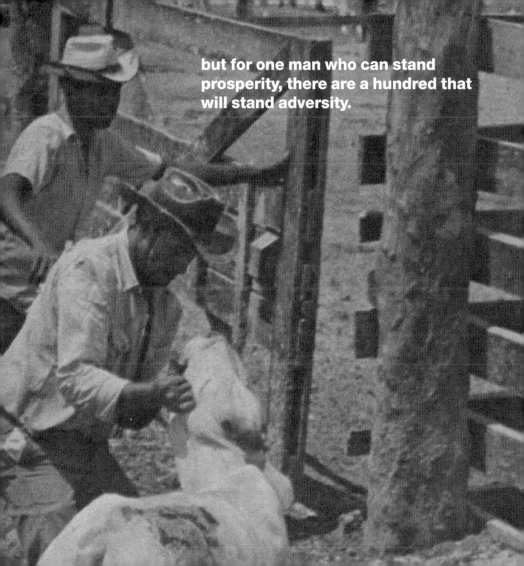

but for one man who can stand prosperity, there are a hundred that will stand adversity.

got

Music should be something that makes you a move inside and outside.

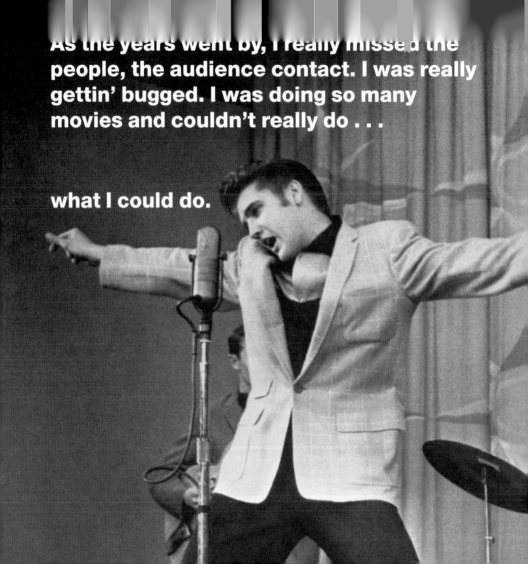

As the years went by, I really missed the people, the audience contact. I was really gettin' bugged. I was doing so many movies and couldn't really do . . .

what I could do.

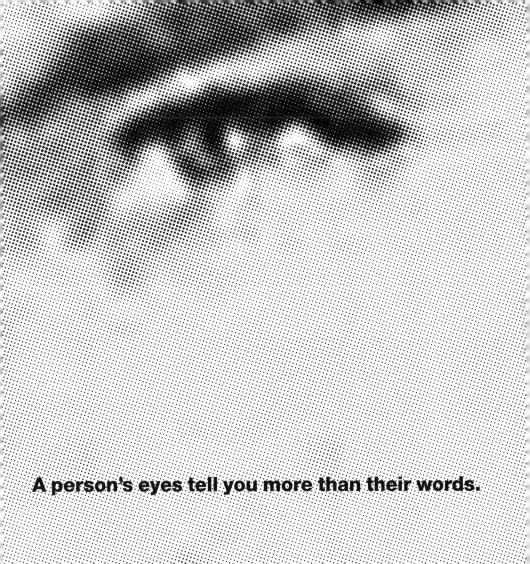

A person's eyes tell you more than their words.

I always felt a little bit lonely—maybe a better word would be "incomplete"—when I was little. But I could tell my mother about it, how I felt, and then the feeling would go away. I suppose it might have been different if my brother had lived. But he didn't live, and I grew up . . .

alone.

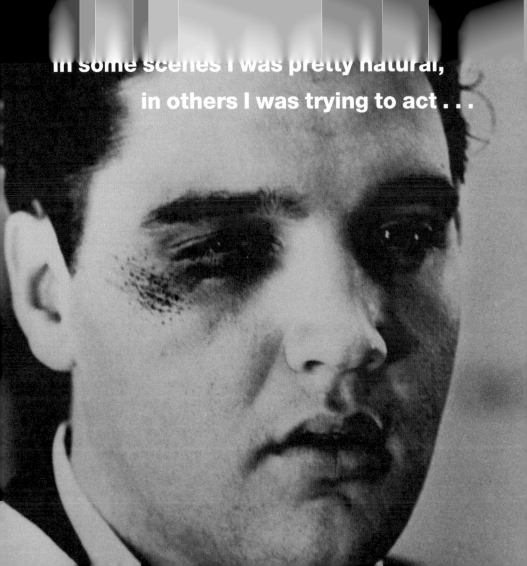

In some scenes I was pretty natural,
in others I was trying to act . . .

and when you start trying to act,

you're dead.

all any kid needs is hope and the feeling he or she belongs. If I could do or say anything that would give some kid I would believe I had contributed something to the world.

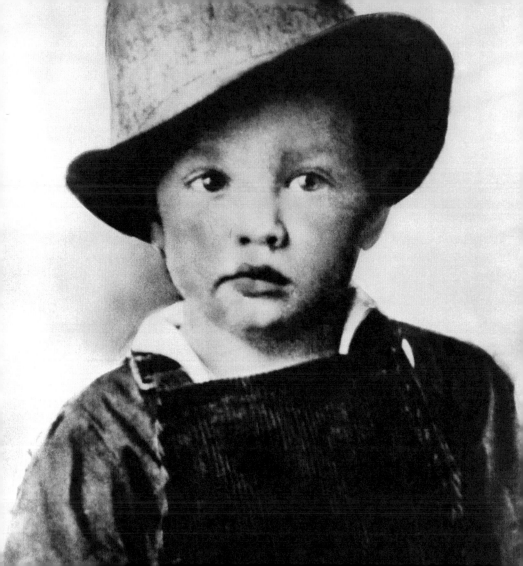

I never felt poor.

There were always shoes to wear and food to eat—yet I knew there were things my parents did without just to make sure I was clothed and fed.

but I've tried never to do anything that

I ain't no saint . . .

would hurt my family or offend God.

jump around

around

In fact, I can't even sing

because it
is
the
way I feel.
with a beat at all if I stand still.

I don't see that any type of music . . .

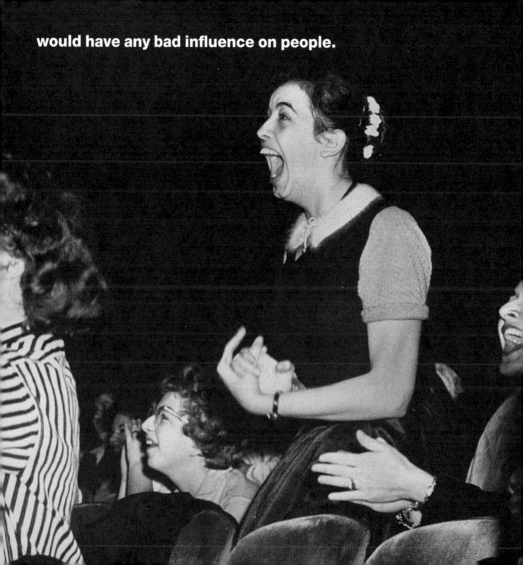

would have any bad influence on people.

I don't believe I'd sing the way
I do if God hadn't wanted me to.

My voice is

God's will, not mine.

Don't criticize what you don't understand, son.

You never walked in that man's shoes.

It's not how much you have that

people look up to, it's who you are.

Some people tap their feet,
some people snap their fingers,
and some people sway back and forth.
I just sorta . . .

do 'em
all
ether,
I guess.'

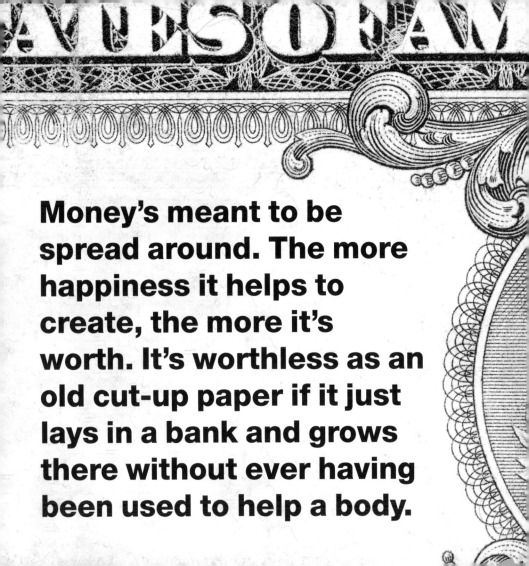

Money's meant to be spread around. The more happiness it helps to create, the more it's worth. It's worthless as an old cut-up paper if it just lays in a bank and grows there without ever having been used to help a body.

I can't figure out what I'm doing wrong.

I know my mother approves of what I'm doing.

People ask me where I got my singing style.
I didn't copy my style from anybody.

I've got nothing in con
except that we both sing . . .

mon with Johnnie Ray,

if you want to call it singing.

You only pass through this life once;

you don't come back for an encore.

Do what's right for you . . .

as long as it don't hurt no one.

My m

she never really wanted anything. She stayed the same through it all. There are a lot of things that's happened since she passed away. I wish she could have been around to see them. It would have made her very happy and proud . . .

other,

but that's life, and I can't help it.

When rock 'n' roll dies out another type of emotional music is going to take its place.

When the audience looks like they're enjoying it, you put more into it.

I've tried to live a straight, clean life and not set any kind of a bad example.

'Til we meet you

again, may God bless you.

Adiós.

Side **2** Mono

NL 89107

THE ELVIS PRESLEY
SUN COLLECTION

1. **Mystery Train** (Parker/Phillips)
   Carlin Music Corp.
2. **I Forgot To Remember To Forget** (Kesler/Feathers)
   Dick James Music Ltd
3. **I'll Never Let You Go** (Little Darling) (Wakely)
   Peter Maurice Music Co. Ltd./EMI Music
4. **I Love You Because** (1st Version) (Leon Payne)
   Bourne Music Ltd
5. **Tryin' To Get To You** (Singleton/McCoy) Carlin

BIEM

GEMA

Moon (Rodgers/Hart) The Big 3 Music
Shelton/Joe Shelton/Si

0316